Broken2Blessed

By Raina Knox

Dedication

I dedicate my book to my Aunt, Carolyn Grace McCants, as a testimony to all those who survived their abusive partners and those who did not. My aunt was a guiding spirit in my life and inspired me into becoming so much of what I am today. I pray that she may continue to rest in peace.

Acknowledgment

To get to the point where I am today, it took the help and guidance of a few special people who never abandoned on me. Chief among them is my mother, who never gave up on me, even when I wanted to give up on myself. Her constant support helped me get through some of the darkest periods of my life, and I will be forever grateful to her.

I would also like to acknowledge my cousin, Leslie Watkins, R.I.P. (5/8/2016).who encouraged me to tell my story in a book; this book. She believed by doing so, I can help other women in the same predicament overcome their abusive relationships too. She told me that I am not a victim, I am a survivor, and that my story can save numerous others into becoming survivors too.

I would also like to acknowledge my sister, Shakiva Sanders and Cousin Demetrius Harris, who always had me and my kids' back and kept us going. They are the best and most supportive loved ones that anyone could have asked for, and it is because of their encouragement that I decided to write this book.

The father of my oldest son, Shaka Hargrove, also

helped me out in more situations than one. He always insured that our son never had to be stuck in a scenario where he had to save his mother. He himself saved me a number of times, which I am deeply grateful to him for.

I also wish to acknowledge my friends, Joynae Jones, Christina Moore, and Easley, who are honestly more like my sisters than my friends. They helped me so much during the most trying of times; especially after I left my abusive relationship and was trying to recover. They incessantly reminded me that I deserved better and helped me believe in myself once again. They are like my personal God sent angels.

Thank you, also, to my hairstylist, Tomeka Premier Boss Hargrett. Who styled my hair and keeps me beautiful on the outside. Thank you to her, and everybody else that assisted me and encouraged me. You all were the lifesaving lighthouse and I was the adrift ship. You guided me towards the safety of the harbor, and helped me become what I am today.

About The Author

Raina Knox is one of the foremost online consultants on domestic violence issues. Her advice for those suffering from the abuse of their partners is widely acclaimed for its effectiveness. It takes one to know one, and as a proud, single mother of six children, she can confirm from her personal experience that nobody hustles harder than a single mother. Being a mother of so many children has not been easy for her over the years, but she has managed to successfully pull through every challenge thrown her way.

She thanks God every day that she does not look like what she has been through for so many years. Indeed, she has weathered many struggles during her time in her hometown Dayton, Ohio, many of which are absolutely shocking to those who are not yet aware of how horrifying domestic violence has the potential to be. Her relationship reached the epitome of how bad such abuse can get.

She was a long-term teacher for Dayton Public Schools for seven years. She then went on to work at some great Fortune 500 companies like, Metlife Insurance, GE Card Services (Fraud Department) and Medaco Pharmacy to name just a few of the many prestigious organizations on her resume. Her professional life could very well be described as a success.

When she lived in her hometown, when she moved she ended up being an independent contractor for more Fortune 500 firms. She worked for these companies from home and after fifteen years of stellar Customer Service and being in Management, she started an online business, '*Pretty Gurlz Hu$tle LLC*'. In addition to this, Raina is also a credit repair consultant

Raina is widely considered to be an inspiring woman for domestic violence victims, but she mostly prefers to try and inspire others. In this respect, she has started a movement called #Rainainspires where she wants to be able help others, especially if they are trying to leave there abusive partner.

Her chief-most desire is to inspire people to work their way towards a better future. She simply wants someone to tell her that because of her efforts, they did not give up. Raina currently resides in Atlanta, where she works day in and day out, making sure her kids have a better life than her. This is on top of her extensive efforts to assist random victims online with their violent relationships. However, this does not mean that she does not find time for hobbies. She enjoys bowling, skating amusement parks and attending family events. So now you know how you can strike up a conversation with her if you ever need to.

Preface

Raina Knox is a survivor of domestic violence, who has written this book to give other women that are in a similar predicament as her the courage to overcome their struggles. She hopes that this book will be able to save the lives of those who are in danger by helping them help themselves.

After her horrifying time with her ex-boyfriend, including a near-death experience, she was left with many emotional scars. However, she strived to rise above them and build a life for herself that she deserves. Today, she has started her own online business, *'Pretty Gurlz Hu$tle LLC'*, which she uses as an example to inspire other women into leaving their abusive partners.

She knows firsthand, from her own abusive relationship, how difficult it can be to take the first step towards doing what is necessary. Hence, she wrote this book with the explicit function to spur those who are hesitant into taking action. Using its guidance, women stuck in toxic households will not only learn what they should do to escape, but exactly why as well so that they understand the importance of doing so. The main objective of this book is to help those women in abusive relationships that do not know what to do, providing them with a clear path towards a better future.

Contents

Page Left Blank Intentionally

Chapter 1

Raina's Wakeup Call

"What I survived might have killed you."

-Anonymous

Every person who has ever lived on this planet has a purpose that they are intended to fulfil. However, all of our lives are filled with hardships and attaining the purpose that we are meant to fulfil becomes cumbersome as a result.

Just like any other human being, I too have been subjected to the misfortunes of life. However, the experiences I have had to date have only helped me become stronger. This is not to say that I have never had it easy or I went through whatever problem came my way, headstrong and unscathed. There were times when I just did not know what to do. This is perhaps the reason why I had the idea to bring to everyone's attention the kind of suffering and abuse many women go through. Not everyone is born strong, and not all of us who have been abused can get out of their situation as a strong person; that too without any help. They need people to guide them on how to be stronger and how to fight against all odds. They needed to be shown the way that can help them win the battle they are facing.

In order for you to be able to understand what goes on in a woman's life who has been abused, I want to first tell you my story. I am a 39 years old single mother to six children who has faced countless adversities. The traumatic incidents that unfolded in my life tore it apart and left me in a devastating state. I was mentally and physically abused regularly by my partner, and had to battle with the demons left behind by domestic violence for over a decade.

Maybe after all this suffering, God had a plan for me; a much better one. After suffering through this torment, I decided to move me and my five children into my mother's place in Atlanta, who showed unconditional support and love to me.

I progressed and worked even harder than before to

build a happier and healthier life for myself and my children. Now, from where I stand, I can see that I have been somewhat successful in what I wanted to achieve. I am an entrepreneur that has successfully started an online business known as *'Pretty Gurlz Hu$tle LLC'.*

It would not be wrong to say that what I went through is a part of my life that should not go unnoticed. I was viciously victimized for 10 years by men I put all my trust in. I tried to love them, but they abused me whenever they got the chance to. A man who had betrayed me hundreds of times was the father of two of my children, and it was because of my children that I tried to tolerate him.

It all started from the time when I opened my eyes into a suffocating world, yearning for love, as well as financial and mental support. My mother was a single parent and how she brought me up on her own is a story in itself. I vividly remember those days when she used to come home late because she was doing overtime to earn extra money. Survival for both of us did not come easy, and with all the financial burden to handle, I mentally matured before my age.

Going to high school and getting better education was

my only escape from the bitter realities of life. During my teenage years, this is how I came across a person who was lovable and had a charming personality; someone who I have grown up with.

Due to my quest for someone who I liked, I came across my first love when I was only 18 years old. While he was finishing his high school, I was getting admitted to college and eventually, we got closer. For a broken girl like me who never had a male figure in her life, crossing paths with him just felt right. He was a person who would always take good care of me and helped me out from time-to-time.

More than half of my life revolved around him, and in due course, I got attached to him. By 2003, I got into a relationship with him since he seemed like such a good person to me. I had no idea that he would cause so much destruction for me in the future. Within the following years, he showed me his true colors. However, he was not the only one who made me hate my life.

Most of the men I encountered in my life abused me in the same manner. I was subjected to their constant mood swings. Whatever the reason was, men with whom I was romantically involved eventually got more demanding and tried to control every aspect of my personal and professional life. All of this came as a shock to me, but I was inclined to work it out with all of them because of the children.

I thought that having our own kids will make things better between us, but these men proved me wrong once again. Soon, things started to align themselves and I realized that the people I was dating had unresolved childhood issues for a very long time.

My messed up relationships were an open secret for my friends and family members. Almost all of them used to ask me why I was staying with them in the first place, and urged me to leave them as soon as possible.

As much as everyone was imploring me to move on, a part of me was asking me to hold on, just for the sake of my children. Unlike me, who had to grow up without a father, I wanted them to have a complete family with a father figure. I desired the best for them and did not want them to have a miserable life like mine. So I tried my best to make a compromise, but the physical and mental abuse I was going through started getting worse.

Apart from that, I was making it obvious to my kids'

father that I did not want him around me or my kids from time to time, but he was reluctant to leave my home. I knew that he had some unresolved issues since childhood, and could not care less about anybody in his life; including his own child. I knew he was lashing out on me because of his personal insecurities and impulsive behavior. Even the thought of this happening to me made me cry and I did not know how to feel any better.

By then, I realized that this excruciating pain would be the end of me. Every single day looked like a mental challenge for me and all of my self-confidence was gone. I had trouble sleeping at night because of the emotional and physical abuse I was going through. This unceasing fear and anxiety led to the birth of depression, which was extremely difficult for me to recover from. In the long run, I lost all control over my senses and accepted the fact that things will remain like this forever.

My mother was the only person who made me feel a little better, because of which I used to share even the tiniest of details about my life with her. When I told her about what I was going through, and how my partner was abusing me, she advised me to inform the police immediately. She further told me that this was not a situation to be overlooked. It was a serious form of domestic violence and I knew what she was telling me to do was my only option. However even the police was unable to remove him from my residence.

This encounter with the authorities infuriated him even more, and he assured me that if he could not have me, then no one can. I did not know what I ever did to him that made him so violent towards me, but his violent acts disgusted me. The only thing I ever thought about was how to get rid of him, but I was not thinking straight as suicide seemed like the only solution to this unending nightmare.

When I needed my friend's support the most, they were nowhere to be found. This made it even harder for me to get out of the abusive relationships. Time flew by, and I was eventually in the tenth year of getting abused by men like him. Sacrificing my inner self-esteem for the sake of my family, and fearing whatever I imagined could be worse than this, wasted 10 years of my healthy life. Even then, I was forced to act like a normal person and put a smile on my face whenever in public. However, things were not the same anymore. I became numb because of the continuous domestic violence, which was now an inseparable part of me. I do not know how I managed to keep faith in God, but

I sincerely believed my miseries would end sooner or later.

During that time, I was the manager at a reputable retail store and my partner used to pick me up from there. When it was time to go home, my partner was late to pick me up, as usual. I was exhausted because of work and did not want to argue with him, so I waited for him to show up. I waited and waited, but he just would not show up. So I called my Aunt out of frustration and told her that if he will do this to me one more time, I will call the police to put up a restraining order against him. Although I said it out of frustration and would love to see him behind bars, I was too fatigued to contact the police and complain against him.

Two hours later, he finally showed up to pick me. When I got in the car, I could see that he had no shame or guilt for making me wait for so long and acted like nothing had happened at all. I was pissed to the core, but was in no mood to start an argument, so I sat quietly and kept looking outside the window. He could see that something was bothering me and later asked what was wrong with me. Without even looking at him, I shut him off by saying I am just tired and do not feel like talking.

On our way back home, I was startled to see all the police gathered around my house. There were policemen with shotguns at the front door, as well as at the back. I knew I was not the one who called them, but realized who might have. It was a sign from God; He was helping me through my Aunt, who must have been the one who called the police after I spoke with her. Deep inside, I was happy about it because my Aunt did something I was always scared of doing on my own.

He was equally shocked to witness all of this as he did not see this coming at all. It was evident that he was fuming about it and asked me why I would call the police on him. From what I knew about his mentality, he would not trust my words, even if I told him the truth. However, I was not expecting what he did right afterwards.

He turned the car around the street in a hurry and pulled out a gun he must have hidden somewhere inside. All this happened in a matter of seconds, and as he drove towards the interstate, he pointed the gun at me. He threatened to kill me in an enraged tone; that he will kill me today since I asked for this myself. I went hysterical when he said that, and was utterly out of words when he pointed the gun to my face. I swore upon my life that I did not call the police and had no idea about what had just happened. Even my continuous pleading did not stop him from pulling the trigger, but my faith in God was restored as the safety was on and the bullet did not come out.

For 10 years of my life, I went through so much because of him and other men, who made me lose my faith in humanity. I was traumatized after facing all of this, but there was still a sign of hope left as the police were chasing after us. We were on the highway when the police finally caught up to us, and all I could think about was getting away from him. So I jumped out of the car on the highway as soon as I saw the chance. It was him who had made my life unbearable and it was him who went out of his mind and did not even think twice before pulling a gun on me. When he abducted me, I realized that I had to put an end to this since I had had enough of this agonizing life.

At the time of my abduction, I already had two children; an older son, thank God he never witnessed me being abused, and a younger daughter, both of whom were very small at that time. They are both much older now and are living a healthier life; the one I always wished for them. After that incident, my mother asked me to move in with her. But it took me a few years to actually follow through.

Even I was looking to start over with a new life from scratch in a place where the memories of my past will haunt me less. With my children safely in my custody, I went to live with my mother in Atlanta, who helped me the most with upbringing my kids and helping me with my financial needs.

On the other hand, my boyfriend was fined and went to prison for a non-related charge where he was supposed to spend two years. He served his time and got out within 18 months. I could not be happier about karma getting the worst of him, and no wonder Jesus Christ had blessed me with His divine power.

I tried to overcome my past with the constant encouragement given by my mother, who persuaded me to live a normal life like I used to before he came into my life. I was a homeless mother with two kids to feed, but my mother was the one who motivated me that anything is possible if I put my heart into it. It is not like I recovered from the ten years' worth of mental and physical abuse within months. It took me almost 5 years to forget the existential pain he instilled within me. It was slow recovery, but I tried to engage myself by focusing on my work and children.

I worked from home whenever I could because I have had remarkable expertise in the customer service department, where I have years of experience. Healing from my past was a slow process, but I took gradual steps towards it by working online day and night.

Now, I am at that stage in life where I am working on assisting those people who can relate to my previous sufferings. I knew how suicidal I got and deeply feel for others who are going through the same mental and physical torture. Initially, it was my mother's idea to not give up on life and help others from feeling the same. One of the lessons I have learnt is that the strongest people are the ones who need the most help. Now, it is my sole motive to help them become the strongest and happiest; just as I did.

Furthermore, I am running my small business as mentioned above, and am the CEO. My movement 'Raina Inspires' encourages people to never give up as they have the power to change their lives if they want to. Not a day goes by when I do not inspire people who had roadblocks, just like I did, keeping them from maintaining their good habits to overcome depression. I personally know how hard recovering from torment can be, but the key to a happier life is having a healthy mental state in order to make the recovery process easier.

Not just that, but I am also starting a Raina Inspires foundation in this fight to save people who are lost and have no hope left to live. Right now, I am a 39 year old single mother who works from home and has started an online business known as *'Pretty Gurlz Hu$tle LLC'*. Apart from that, I am working on God's mission of helping out those who are waiting for guidance from His servants; people like me.

I help people in getting their credit restored and back on track. I want to encourage any woman who has ever experienced the same to keep moving forward in life at all costs. After moving to Atlanta and recovering from the dangerous abduction perpetrated by my kids' father, life has definitely turning around for me. Not just that, but life had really given me a second chance and I am no longer a victim, but a survivor.

I am proud to mention that my oldest child was awarded a full ride scholarship to continue playing football at Bowling Green State University. Moreover, I am fortunate enough to have five more children whom I love. I will forever remain humble and thankful to God for blessing me with this brighter side in life. I am stronger than ever and wish the same for every other women out there.

Chapter 2

Never Silence Domestic Violence

"Don't let someone who did you wrong, make you think like there's something wrong with you. Don't devalue yourself because they didn't value you. Know your worth even if they don't."

-Anonymous

Whether it be psychological or physical abuse, many people have been a victim to it for years. It is almost uncommon to hear that everybody is happy with their partners and have never been humiliated in any way by them. Irrespective of age, ethnicity, gender, and religion, humankind has abused one another in multiple horrific ways. People have been exploited, molested, tortured, sexually manipulated and mentally harmed more than once.

When this violence is inflicted upon a partner, it is known as '*domestic violence*'.

Just like me, there are many other people who have been targeted by their loved ones. People who have lost their will to live because their partners did not treat them well. All our lives, we dream of falling in love with someone who will understand us and love us unconditionally. Someone who would listen out to us and cater to all of our needs. Ask yourself, would you like to live the rest of your lives with someone who would mistreat you, harm you, and molest you, then in exchange demand your unconditional love? Do you not think that is skewed? Would you even like to be in their presence? At times, when a person becomes helpless and has a hard time finding their way out of this situation, they eventually become completely numb to the violence. It is almost like Stockholm syndrome, where the victim no longer even realizes that they are being mistreated.

What Domestic Violence Really Is?

Typically, domestic violence refers to the type of violence a person experiences from a spouse or partner within their household. According to the National Domestic Violence Hotline organization, this term is also known as the Intimate Partner Violence (IPV) or relationship abuse. Analogous to any other type of violence, it begins with irrational behavior or action. It is then followed up by a partner inflicting excruciating harm upon their significant other in order to dominate them in an intimate relationship. It is done to solidify control and power over another person, and make them suffer to an extent that they lose all hope for themselves.

If you are thinking that only women are the victim of this, then you are wrong. There is no gender discrimination when it comes to domestic violence: men are victims to it too. This kind of violence usually starts surfacing only after a person gets involved in a relationship seriously. This is because once a person gets bound, they tend to tolerate the emotional and physical torture. From the victims who are dating someone that cannot control their anger, to those who have been married for years to an abusive sadist, anyone can someday find themselves in such a situation. Oftentimes, people have this perception that only illiterate and unprivileged people tend to bully their partners, but this is far from the case in real life. People of every other socioeconomic background and educational level can be violent towards their partners. It is a huge emotional and physical trauma for the people who are going through domestic abuse since they assumed the person who they were tying the knot with would be someone who would genuinely cherish them. This sudden betrayal and the subsequent painful memories follow them throughout their life.

But how does this domestic violence even occur? One of the most common factors driving domestic violence is the desire to gain complete control over another person and dominate them. People should realize that being abusive is a learned behavior and is often related to unresolved childhood conflicts. There can be many psychological reasons behind being abusive. Even though these underlying factors are understandable, they should be treated as they in no means justify violent acts. Indeed, many abusers come up with various excuses to satisfy their abnormal behaviors, like getting angry over unimportant things, mental health issues, and substance abuse. However, they do little to actually treat the underlying drivers behind them.

Just to feel superior and dominant over another person, they will use antagonism, fright, guiltiness, indignity, and extortion to manipulate the other person and make them adjust to their own sexual and mental needs.

This alarming scenario is getting more common by the day as the abusers do not even think before threatening, hurting, or abusing their partners in open spaces.

Here, it is important to note that statistically more women are likely to become a victim of domestic violence than men. Based on the data, one out of three women experience abuse in their entire life. Mostly, the victims do not get the liberty to do what they wish for and are repeatedly forced to do things they never wanted to. For that reason, they get accustomed to fulfil the different needs of the abuser, even though they get sexually and emotionally violent. They do so just to feel good about themselves and make their partner understand who 'runs' the household, even if they are not the primary breadwinner.

Types Of Domestic Violence

There is no justifying the heinous act of exploiting someone verbally or physically. This can result in a lot of complications for the person's trust in other people. Their self-confidence collapses, and their power to make decisions diminishes. It is indeed a terrible thing to have your confidence crushed to an extent that you are unable to defend yourself when any type of abuse is hurled at you. It is important that you know what specific type of abuse that you are, or someone you know is, going through. Knowledge of this will lead you to finding the perfect solution for it.

Although this subject will be discussed extensively in the upcoming chapters, in order to give you an idea on what possibilities exist in the realms of domestic violence, it is best that you be introduced to the concept beforehand. A majority of people think that domestic violence comprises of physical attacks suffered by individuals. But this is only one of the types of the numerous abusive behaviors displayed by the aggressor. Indeed, there are several categories in which this abusive behavior is divided into, and every single one of them has its own devastating side effects. There are many types of abuse, but the most prevalent ones are listed below.

Wanting Control Over Another Person

When in a relationship, the abuser displays controlling and manipulative behavior just to channel out their dominance over their significant other. You may feel that a person is being overly protective at first, but the person may end up abusing you physically or verbally when their *'conditions'* are not met. This type of abusive behavior is exhibited out of fear of letting the partner do what they want to and losing authority over them. Such people are mentally challenged and narrow-minded. Many men tragically think this way because they want their wives and girlfriends to stay committed to them. Their insecurity makes them over possessive and they will not let their partner live in peace.

For instance, they will keep a check on their partner's phone activity and travels. It is not easy for them to give any freedom to their partner due to their own affliction, and they hardly allow them to do the things they want to.

Women do not even get the choice of wearing those clothes they want to. Instead, they are either coerced into dressing in a seductive manner, so the abuser can parade them around, or completely cover up their body, so that it deflects any attention.

Another form of this excessive control is invading the privacy and personal space of their partner. The abusive partner tries to control every single detail and intrudes into even the smallest of facets of the victim's life. This is all in an effort to convince the victim to believe that they are worthless without the abuser so that they completely depend on them to survive in future despite the constant violence.

Physical Abuse

As cited by the AMEND Workbook for Ending Violent Behavior, physical abuse happens when a person settles on showing physically aggressive behavior from time-to-time. This is another way of demonstrating control over their partner, who is then physically harmed on a frequent basis. Women suffer more from it and live under the constant threat of physical abuse for most of their lives. Physical abuse has no boundaries and can be in the form of;

- Not letting the victim fulfil their physical needs, like sleeping, eating, shopping, travelling, medical treatment, and more.
- They are also denied effective treatment if they get sick or injured because the abuser locks them inside the house.
- Hitting, slapping, kicking, biting, punching, pulling, choking, pinching, beating, stabbing, drowning, burning, using heavy objects for beating, torturing them with deadly weapons, threatening to kill them, and more.
- Forcing their partners to stay in the house and not leave without them at any cost.
- Pushing them off the stairs and using different inanimate objects during a fight.
- Throwing things at them out of anger and feeling satisfied after physically abusing them.

Sexual Abuse

Sexual abuse is yet another common form of domestic violence where the abuser uses sex to force the other person to fulfil their sexual demands. Engaging in sex without consent is just the start. The perpetrator forces their partner to perform numerous extreme sex acts and subjugates them to pain during intercourse. Herein, sexual abuse can be inflicted verbally, physically, or both.

- The abusers force their girlfriends or wives to have sex with them. If they refuse, then they will do it forcefully; essentially raping them.

- At times, they will want to see their partner have sex with others without their consent. This is also done to solicit favors from those who they are '*permitting*' to rape their spouse.

- Many abusive men also force their partners to get involved in prostitution and have sex with sexually frustrated men without their will.

- Passing disgraceful and offensive comments on their sexuality, criticizing them for not being good enough, and insulting them in a violent manner.

- Restricting the victims to stay in the house and function like a sex doll, just so they get pleased by them.

- Threatening to leave their partners by having affairs with other women and bringing them home to infuriate them.

- Not having sex with them or giving them attention, holding them hostage for control mechanisms.

Emotional Abuse

According to Michael Lindsay's AMEND Workbook for Ending Violent Behavior, emotional abuse is termed as any behavior that makes the victim feel insecure about themselves in any way. Victims get criticized on a normal basis and due to the continuous humiliation, brainwashing, and manipulation, they lose their own sense of identity.

The abusers do so just to torch the self-esteem of their partners, they weaken their self-confidence as well.

The following behaviors are examples of being emotionally abusive;

- Humiliating their parents in public and negatively commenting on their dressing sense, way of talking, and overall posture.
- Using abusive language and hateful words against them in front of others, as well as in private.
- Verbally bullying and mentally torturing them to the extent that they develop severe anxiety and depression.

- Causing emotional stress and frightening them in order to create an opening to begin harming them sexually and physically.

- Blackmailing them in order to make their partners obey them as much as they can.

- Passing ironic statements to make the victim feel more insecure about themselves, like doing the opposite of what they said earlier.

- Lying to their victims and not trusting them over small things. This may include blaming them for any and all distresses in the house, making false accusations about them, and suspecting them of having affairs with other people.

- Not listening out to them and overlooking what their partners want, just to cause them discomfort.

- Consistently behaving in a disturbing way and showing gestures that violate the self-worth of the victims.

- Having bad intentions for them and messing with their mental health by saying that they are incapable of living normally.

- Making their partners to abuse narcotics with them, forcing them to do drugs and alcohol.

- Not permitting their partners to practice their religious beliefs and using those religious beliefs as an excuse to abuse the victims even more.

- Calling them with abusive names, and telling them they deserve all of these hateful and abusive remarks.

Other than that, the victims are economically stalked as well, where the abuser keeps a check on the expenditures of their partners. For that reason, the victims act in a timid and frightened manner when it comes to spending money on themselves. They do not even shop for basic things, unless absolutely necessary. They become liable to answer to the abuser, who has the dominance over the financial income and expenditure of the house.

Some of the most evident signs of being in an abusive relationship can be;

- Shattering your self-confidence by saying things in a demeaning way.

- Telling you that you are unable to have command over a particular thing or activity.

- Not letting you spend money on your own and restricting access to said money.

- Being over possessive and jealous of the people you are in touch with and keeping an eye on the people you are spending time with.

- Telling you in a firm tone that you are not allowed to meet your friends and family members.

- Never respecting your opinions and always insulting you in private, as well as in public.

- Taking away the money earned by you and not letting you have control over a single penny that you have earned.

- Making you feel like a dependent person who is incapable of making decisions on their own.

- Threatening to inflict pain if you do not do things according to them.

- Neglecting the efforts you have made for them.

- Shouting at you and taunting you for not being good enough or completely perfect.

- Not permitting you to do what you prefer, instead asking you to do things which will satisfy their sexual and physiological urges.

- Showing dominance over you and giving life threats in an aggressive and belittling tone.

- Frightening you with knives, guns, and other deadly weapons if you do not fulfil their needs.

- Pressurizing you to have sex with them, even when you do not feel like it.

- Making you do sexual activities that make you uncomfortable.

The list does not end here; far from it in fact. We will learn more about the types and signs of this domestic violence in the upcoming chapters.

Facts And Figures Of Domestic Violence According To The National Statistics Domestic Violence Fact Sheet

Domestic violence is not just limited to women; men face it as well. Approximately 20 people per minute suffer from domestic violence in the United States alone. This equals to more than 10 million women and men who eventually fall victim of this sexual, mental, and physical harassment (Black, M.C., Basile, K.C., Breiding, M.J., Smith, S.G., Walters, M.L., Merrick, M.T., Chen, J. & Stevens, M. (2011). The National Intimate Partner and Sexual Violence Survey: 2010 summary report).

As mentioned above, one in three women become a victim of this violence, whereas one in four men have gone through the same more than once in their lifetime. The list of victims and survivors goes on and on when it comes to domestic violence. However, more women are vulnerable to become prey to it and lose their identity after being in an intimate relationship.

According to domestic violence statistics, 20,000 phone calls (on an average basis) are placed on domestic violence hotlines nationwide. Victims do not know from where they should get help, and they end up calling on these hotlines to save their lives. Actually, this is the sole purpose of these hotlines, which are active 24/7 all around the world.

This Intimate Partner Violence is spread worldwide and lately, it has been accounted for almost 15% of all the violent crimes being done on a daily basis. This is not something that should go unnoticed and unfortunately, the rate of destruction caused by the domestic violence may increase in the upcoming years.

This is probable if thorough measures are not taken into account. Rape, stalking, verbal, and physical violence are some of the most sensitive issues that should be brought to the attention of the higher authorities and into the public discourse. Quite alarmingly, it has been noted that 19.3 million women and 5.1 million men in the United States have been subjected to stalking within their lifetime. This is not normal at all and is something that needs to be worked on.

It has also been reported that 60.8% of the women and 43.5% of men have been a victim of trust issues and unnecessary stalking by their current or former partners.

As this domestic violence will continue, psychological or mental health issues will arise with the passage of time. People who have been exposed to this know how messed up their life gets once they start living in an abusive relationship.

Domestic violence leads to mental and health related problems like PTSD and cardiovascular diseases developing. In addition to that, all types of violent behavior is directly related to a higher rate of depression and suicide among the victims.

In terms of the economic implications of all this, it can be seen that almost 142 women were murdered in their workplace by abusers in the years between 2003 and 2008. This is equivalent to 78% of women who have been killed after being domestically victimized.

What people do not understand is the sensitivity of this subject. Any kind of domestic abuse should not be neglected as it is a much bigger problem than you think. It is very much like an iceberg; what one sees on the surface does not even come close to being equal to what is beneath it. As soon as the victim falls under the trap of their abusive partner, they start facing psychological and physical health issues that do not just stop at depressive and suicidal attempts.

What Are The Implications Of

Domestic Violence

It is evident that there are no positive side effects of causing distress to your partner in the household. While it is understood that the negative side effects vary, if the victim keeps on tolerating the violent behavior for a long period of time, they become vulnerable to various types of psychological and physical disorders.

Staying in such toxic relationships has their own drawbacks, which messes up the physical, mental, and social wellbeing of the bullied victim. For your knowledge, some of the commonly found implications of domestic violence are listed below;

- Majority of the people who have been victimized for a long period of time tend to suffer from heart conditions, asthma, chronic pains in different parts of the body, migraines, and more. Also, their condition gets worse if they get exposed to the stress of it for a longer period than the body is designed to deal with.

- When a victim is incessantly abused, they somehow lose faith in living out a happy and healthy life. When this happens, they start developing psychological disorders as their cognitions start acting up in a negative manner. In this condition, the victim starts stressing out about the relationship they are in, as a result going through Post Traumatic Stress Disorder, depression and anxiety attacks.

- At times, the victims try to run away from the reality and get accustomed to consuming alcohol and doing drugs in an abnormal manner.

- Not just the depression and anxiety, but the sleeping pattern of the victims get disoriented as well, and that leaves them sleep deprived.

- These chronic emotional problems also transfer to the next generation as well, who then inherit the impacts of domestic abuse.

- Physical side effects of getting abused are bruises, broken bones, complications in pregnancy, sexually transmitted diseases, gynecological disorders, and cuts.

- The victim also suffers from low self-esteem and loses all hope in the future and refrains from putting their trust in someone else again.

- Amidst all of this, the victim finds solitude in committing suicide, just to get over with the domestic violence once and for all.

- Fear of intimacy also shows up, where the victims do not find sexual acts or intimate behaviors comforting at all.
- Victims also isolate themselves from their close family members, friends, and other people they normally interact with.

These are only a few of the negative side effects of the sufferers, who become a victim of these disorders for longer than usual. It should be noted that domestic violence has been happening since time immemorial and will not be eliminated until and unless we get serious about it. Be it the physical symptoms or the mental ones, one needs to have full knowledge about domestic violence to efficiently deal with it. In fact, domestic violence has more to it than the factors discussed above, and it will be studied further in detail.

Chapter 3
The Beginning

"Maybe the best proof that the language is patriarchal is that it oversimplifies feeling."

-Jeffrey Eugenides

Domestic violence is a complex issue that we have been surrounded with for decades. It has been here for a long time; as long as the Roman Empire, when women were considered the property of men. We have already discussed that more women than men become a victim of this domestic violence ever since its origin. In order to understand how domestic violence penetrated and took birth, let us look at it from the beginning.

History Of Domestic Violence

As far as I have studied, the history of domestic violence is as timeless as the history itself. Abusing women in different forms like rape, sexual exploitation, mental and physical torture has penetrated society for a long time. These various forms of demoralization have been a part of different German infused camps, pirated slave ships in North America, and the World War II where various brothels were made. These brothels were occupied with women who were supposed to comfort men in any way possible, and this has been a ritual since then. This is no wonder as men and women both were illiterate back then and women had no choice left but to obey the prejudicial demands of the men in charge.

If we talk about the history of domestic violence in Greece, we would easily find various articles where laws were made regarding having the male head for the entire household. This gave an open ground to men, who thought that controlling and abusing women was something they could rightfully do back then. For this reason, women had no choice left but to obey the male guardian they were made answerable to. This circle of life, in return, led to the never-ending upsurge of domestic violence.

However, Greeks were not the only ones with issues regarding domestic violence. The practice of husbands abusing their women was also common in the Roman Empire, where women were physically abused, thrown out of their homes, divorced by the choice of their husbands, and murdered by the male head of the household. Only the women of the upper class would be heard. They were also permitted to divorce their husbands if the domestic violence crossed its limits. Lower and middle-class women, on the other hand, had no right to question the wrongdoings of their husband and could not even file for a divorce from them.

Even, in the European societies of the Middle Ages, women were not socially allowed to talk about domestic violence or raise their voice against it. They were not allowed to study and were asked to stay away from the political affairs of the state as it was only men's right to educate themselves and run the government.

It is not like women loved setting themselves up for toxic relationships with violent men. In the past, marriages were often arranged by the elders and the future husbands without taking the consent of the women or daughter of the household. Women were supposed to be kept in homes as all they were needed for was to give birth, care for their children, satisfy males' sexual urge, clean the house, and cook food for the family members. They were objectified because of many reasons, mainly to gratify the fragile ego of the men they were dependent upon.

This domestic violence reached its extreme heights in certain cases, where society tried to abuse women in the form of infibulation – this is where a women's genitals' parts, like the clitoris and labia, are stitched up to the edges of the vulva in order to prohibit them from sexual intercourse and has been a norm in African cultures – and cutting off female genitals, which is normally known as female circumcision. Violent acts like these are extreme. Thousands of years have passed and still, the perception of *'women are less valuable than men'* has not changed.

Women would be victimized and assaulted for attending school and never had the privilege to receive higher education as early 1700s. They would be killed and brutally tortured by their own male family members in the name of *'honor killing'*. They would be raped for many reasons, with no particular one being remotely logical. It has been hundreds of years and the majority of the times, women's consent is not taken for premarital sex in some countries. Not only that, but also only men were given sufficient legal rights to raise their opinions and voice whenever they wanted.

This was unlikely the case for women, who were prohibited from serving on juries and having prestigious jobs like other men of the same educational status in the United States. Women were also excluded from voting and were not given the rights they deserved until 1920. This clearly depicts that the domestic violence thousands of women now face had been in this society since long ago.

It has been in this society that this view developed; that women come under men status-wise. This unjustified delusion of the society invigorated domestic violence and maltreatment of women. In spite of the fact that it is a genuine wrongdoing that regularly leaves lasting scars, aggressive behavior at home has not generally been taken into account by higher authorities; like police or courts. The reason for this will be the battered thought that your partner has all the rights in the world to do whatever he wants to in order to have dominance over you. Even some of the most literate and successful men in our society think that their life partner is more like a property they own – someone who is not a real, breathing human. Our society has been corrupted with this mentality for many years and when the higher authorities are unwilling to take action, who will go to take a stand?

However, this perception eventually changed when multiple cases of domestic violence were highlighted. One of which was the 1972's case of Ruth Bunnell, who was murdered by her husband – her significant other – and no one took notice of that, least of all the police. This injustice was then publicized on the media and people could not tolerate the irresponsibility of the higher authorities.

Another case was brought up in the United States in 2000, where a woman named Maria Macias was killed by her husband with whom she was on bad terms. She repeatedly told the police on several occasions that she needed protection from her husband, but she was not acknowledged officially. All of this was even put on record, yet she could not protect herself from her evil husband. It was later recognized that the police department actually failed to respect the rightful protection request made by her and insure that she was safe.

These are not the only cases where the rights of women were denied. When public perceptions finally began moving towards modernization, several other women like Maria started raising their voice against injustice happening to them and by the end of the 1980s, various police departments started taking serious actions against the suspects of domestic violence. Whenever the police officers were provided with real evidence of abuse, serious actions were taken.

Changes like these around the world raised the awareness about the topic of domestic violence. As soon as the problems like these were recognized as a criminal offense, victims were provided with qualitative safety measures to effectively control the situation.

How To Know If Your Partner Is Abusive To You

At the beginning of the relationship, it might be difficult to understand that the other person has the capability to abuse you at a later point in life. For this reason, identifying the early signs of domestic violence can help you avoid abuse.

The easiest possible solution to knowing the signs of domestic violence could be by asking yourself the following questions;

- Is your spouse trying his best to control you?
- Do you feel uncomfortable around him, in public and in private?
- Does he call out names that are offensive and disrespectful?
- Does he keep track of every single thing you do in front of him and in his absence?
- Does he place any critical or judgmental remarks on the way you dress up and the people you meet on your own?
- Are you allowed to use the car and shop on your own without asking your husband for the car keys or money from time-to-time?
- Do you share the same liberty your husband has in order to spend the money that both of you or your husband is earning?
- Does he force you to have sex with him without your consent?

- How many times did he ignore your opinion in front of others or not give you the chance to speak up?
- Has he started to initiate acts of abuse, like throwing things at you or mentally torturing you, by being over-possessive?

The list of behaviors to interpret and determine whether your spouse is abusive or not is endless. There are many symptoms that tell a person if they are subjected to domestic violence or not. The most important thing is to recognize these early symptoms before it gets way too serious and more harmful for you.

There is an official website known as AARDVARC Its full form is '*An Abuse, Rape, Domestic Violence Aid and Resource Collection*'. On this site, awareness of domestic violence and a number of warning signs have been given for friends, family and coworkers. This is to help them recognize any of the signs of domestic violence being shown on the victims in their circle. In addition, when more people will have awareness of what is happening to the people around them, they will try to help them out in any way possible for them.

With the help of this site, the victims and the general public will be informed about the various dynamics of the abusive relationships they are a part of. Not only that, but also the victims here are encouraged to stand up for themselves and realize that what is happening to them is unfair and illegal.

Ending or getting out of a toxic relationship depends on the willingness of the victim. Some of the victims' self-esteem gets brutally shattered and they fear the consequences of raising their voice against the injustice. Recognizing these signs on your own or being told by others will assist you in saving yourself from an abusive partner as soon as possible. However, you might also be in a tedious situation like myself, being held at gunpoint and brainwashed. Trust me, you do not need to go through that and I hope no one ever should go through what I went through in the past years. So, look around you and do not take even the littlest of signs lightly.

If you are a victim yourself or your close one is being abused domestically, you need to look closely to see what is happening in your surroundings. We tend to get so busy at times that we hardly have the time to ponder on how other people are living their lives. It is our duty to notice our surroundings and the wrongdoings in it.

For instance, if you see someone having a bruised eye or sore tooth, ask what went wrong with them. If you do not ask, you will never be able to relieve them from the constant stress their mind is preoccupied with. This goes for the person who is being abused domestically as well. If you do not talk about the problems you are facing at home and in public with your trusted close ones, you will never be able to recover from the abuse you have been accustomed to. Instead of isolating yourself and giving the power to your spouse to abuse you mentally, physically, sexually, and emotionally, stand up for yourself and do something for your future.

In the upcoming chapter, we will learn about different types of domestic violence in detail. Knowing everything about domestic violence and recognizing different forms of abuse will help the victims escape the toxic relationship they have with their partner so far.

Chapter 4

Recognition Of Abuse

"All problems become smaller when you confront them
instead of dodging them."

-William F. Halsey

Domestic violence can take several shapes and can be recognized in different ways. Typically, there are nine types of domestic abuses, out of which we will be talking about the most common ones. This is important as we should be aware by now about how many prejudicial things are happening to the people around us, especially women.

The world we live in has advanced in many ways, both negative and positive. For that reason, identifying the sensitive matters and knowing how you are being treated is crucial. With the help of the recognition of abuse, you will be able to ascertain the wrongdoings in society and be of help to the victims of domestic violence.

Down below is the detailed explanation of the five most commonly occurring types of domestic abuse;

Physical Abuse

In accordance to the New York State Office of Children and Family Services, the definition of physical abuse is *"non-accidental use of force that results in bodily injury, pain, or impairment. This includes, but is not limited to, being slapped, burned, cut, bruised or improperly physically restrained"*. When an abuser is physically aggressive, there might be a possibility that the victim can lose their life. This is one of the most heartless forms of domestic violence as it leaves the victim despondent.

Such abuse is not only faced by women all over the world, but is suffered by small children as well. However, more women than children or men are physically abused on a daily or weekly basis.

Threats of violence are given by the partner before the act of severe violence, which makes the victim even more afraid than they were before. Some of the examples of physical abuse are;

- Being unable to move out of the house or being tied/locked up inside a room or closet.
- Burning the hands or hair of the victim.
- Beating the body and hitting the face.
- Stabbing with a sharp weapon or shooting with a gun.
- Slapping and pulling hair.
- Making them eat nasty or rotten foods.
- Forcing them to take drugs or excessive amounts of alcohol.
- Making them do abusive things to other people or animals.

This physically aggressive behavior towards you should not be ignored at all. This form of abuse should be highlighted as such an issue will never culminate if it is not being recognized and talked about at the right time.

Sexual Abuse

When any kind of sexual activity is done using force, or without the consent of the partner, then such an activity falls under sexual abuse. Perpetrators use force and cause harm to the self-esteem of the women who are subjected to this sexual abuse from time to time. Taking advantage of the victims without their consent or willingness is a crime, which should be talked about and recognized in the society we are living in.

When a woman is sexually abused and forced to do erotic things, she loses her will to live and is often psychologically and physically tortured during the intercourse. A woman then feels like a sex toy, with whom her partner has been sexually abusive for a long time. Some of the most common reactions to the sexual assault are horror, anxiety, and disbelief.

According to the Encyclopedia of Body Image and Human Appearance, 2012, sexual abuse has been shown to have long-lasting emotional and physical effects on women, regardless of the age when the traumatic incident occurs.

Not just that, but studies have proved that the survivors of sexual abuse face difficulty in putting their trust in relationships. They also suffer from poor self-esteem, sexual problems, and what not.

This sexual assault has been a severe problem since the

dawn of civilization. Thousands of women have become a victim of it and stayed silent afterwards because of fear and guilt. This is unacceptable as such abusive behavior will only inflict more harm in the future if the perpetrator gets off scot-free. These involuntarily sexual experiences have to be dealt with immediately.

Some of the specific sexually abusive behaviors are;

- The person is coerced into non-consensual sex through guilt, manipulation or force.
- Groping, fondling, and touching in a sexual way without the consent of the partner.
- Inflicting pain upon the sensitive parts of the body.
- Forcing them to watch pornographic videos and pictures with them.
- Forcing them to participate in the pornographic activity with a stranger, or even animal.
- Making use of sharp weapons to be sexually explicit.
- Making judgmental sexual comments, or saying shady things.
- Not making love to the partner when they want to.
- Asking them to indulge in prostitution.
- Intentionally divulging the partner to different sexually transmitted infections.

- Forcefully having sex with them a couple of times a day, by themselves and with other people.

Emotional Abuse

Emotional abuse is not only restricted to women nowadays, but teenagers suffer from it too in their surroundings. However, the kind of incessant emotional abuse women go through has long-lasting negative impacts on their mental and physical health.

According to *healthyplace.com*, emotional abuse is *"any act including confinement, isolation, verbal assault, humiliation, intimidation, infantilization, or any other treatment which may diminish the sense of identity, dignity, and self-worth."*

Such an abusive act should be prohibited in our society as this has been a major cause for building up chronic psychological problems. Another name for emotional abuse is *'psychological abuse'* or *'chronic verbal aggression'*, which should be treated as soon as possible.

Some of the symptoms of emotional abuse are;

- Swearing and using abusive names for the partner.

- Bullying them emotionally by torturing their self-esteem.
- Name calling or insulting them in front of others and in private.
- Intentionally ignoring and being intimidating towards their partner.
- Forcing them to become used to the isolation and playing mind games with them.
- Making them feel ashamed and embarrassed by shouting at them.
- Humiliating them from time to time and criticizing them.
- Blaming the victim for not doing things according to the way the abuser wanted them to.
- Not letting their partner eat or drink properly.
- Being disrespectful and not giving them much importance.
- Treating their partner like a servant or a commodity they own.
- Ridiculing their partner, about how they look or other things they do.

This is normally done to show dominance and control over the other person, and making them suffer from emotional agony. When this behavior becomes repetitive, there are higher chances that the victim may lose their initial identity and become someone they were not before. This is a terrible thing to happen to someone who was once under no one's control. Not just that, but the consistent threatening and unsafe environment created can be scary for the victim.

Financial Abuse

In this form of abuse, the partner has full control over the finances. They might not even give you any money at all, which is another type of domestic violence. It has been proven through various surveys on domestic violence that financial abuse occurs in unhealthy relationships, just as much as any other form of domestic abuse.

For your knowledge, there was a study conducted by the Centers for Financial Security, where it was noted that almost 99% of the cases of domestic violence also involved financial abuse of the victims. It was also noted that abusing someone financially is one of the first signs of domestic violence in an intimate relationship.

Such abuse involves having full control or dominance over the finances, and not letting the victim acquire any money or using it without the partner's permission. Not just that, but the victim is usually forbidden from earning money on their own. Not giving the victims full or partial access to make use of financial resources can be disturbing.

Spending money should be everyone's basic right and prohibiting someone from doing so is illegal.

One should know that the examples of financial abuse can vary from situation to situation. Some of the most common circumstances are;

- Prohibiting the victim from using money without their partner's permission.
- Forcing the individual to quit their job or ordering them to start working on a low-wage.
- Not letting the victim spend money on grocery items and other household products
- Having full control over the wages made by them by not letting them buy what they want to.
- Using the victim's bank account or money without their permission, or doing such stuff behind them.
- Blaming the victim for the lost or stolen money.

- Not working on their own, but living off of the victim's salary.
- Wasting the victim's money on drugs and alcohol.
- Not giving access to them by having full control over the bank accounts, credit cards or debit cards.
- Selling or giving the house on rent without taking permission from the victim.
- Forcefully making the victim sign on a paycheck and other legal documents.
- Reading or opening the personal mails of the victim.

Suspecting if your partner is being financially abusive is an important step to take to end the domestic violence. One should know that by not talking about this or highlighting this matter, they would be putting themselves in more danger nonetheless.

Psychological Abuse

Psychological abuse is similar to emotional abuse, but one should not get confused between the two. Identifying psychological abuse is a difficult thing to do as it messes up with the mental cognitions of the victims the most.

However, this form of abuse is just as destructive as any other form of abuse, and is something which should not go unnoticed.

According to the Elder Abuse Prevention Unit, psychological abuse is the *"infliction of mental anguish, involving actions that cause fear of violence, isolation or deprivation, and feelings of shame, indignity or powerlessness (ANPEA)"*.

When a person is abused psychologically, their inner peace gets disturbed and their self-control is shattered. The abuser tries to exert control and dominance over the victim's life by manipulating them in different ways. They could be using this form of abuse to threaten you. They could try to terrorize you by consistently belittling you. Also, they control all aspects of the victim's life by invading their privacy and preventing them from socializing as well.

Down below are some common examples of psychological abuse;

- Use of threats in order to harm the person or their family and friends.

- Giving them warnings and pressurizing them to do something or fulfil their command on time.
- Threatening them over violent acts and making them anxious about getting isolated.
- Stalking the victim or keeping an eye on their physical activities.
- Verbally abusing them.
- Not giving them access to use household items, the car, or other things.
- Not letting them leave the house on their own.
- Not listening to them or taking their opinion on important decisions.
- Making them do those things they never really want to do.
- Shouting at them and not taking care of them if they fall sick or get injured.
- Disturbing them while sleeping by watching television or listening to songs.

Be it psychological abuse, or the other types of domestic violence, it is important to recognize any one of these abuses in order to escape the relationship as soon as possible. Personally, I urge you to speak up about the abuse and look for any possible way to escape it. You can never get out of the domestic violence if you do not identify what is going on around you. Hence, recognizing these different types of domestic abuse is very important. Victims of the domestic abuse in third world countries do not speak up about it because it is considered a norm and they usually have zero awareness about such matters. But this has to be changed and stopped.

These were the five common types of domestic abuse, after which we will be delving deeper into abusive relationships in the next chapter.

Chapter 5
You Deserve Better

"You, yourself, as much as anybody in the entire universe,
deserve your love and affection."

-Buddha

It has been predicted through surveys on domestic violence that 1 in 4 women are vulnerable to becoming victims of this violent act at least once in their lifetime. Even in today's world, people do not discuss a lot about the sufferings of domestic violence, which is still considered as a taboo practice in some places. However, in recent years, this issue has been highlighted on social media, where people have started taking a stand for the victims who are in danger. But one thing the victims will have to understand is that if they will not stand up for themselves, no one else will.

As a victim myself, I know how it feels to detach yourself from your loved ones just because of the constant torture you have to suffer from your partner. This effects your physical, sexual, and mental health, which should not be swept under the rug; ever.

Oftentimes, victims do not understand how valuable their life is and they come under the dominance of their abusive partner. Such a thing should be stopped from the victim's end once and for all.

I know it is not going to be an easy thing to do, but you will have to take the first step in order to get somewhere in life. For that reason, your first step, right here right now, should be to let yourself know that you deserve much more in life than being abused by a mentally sick person.

First and foremost, change the way your cognitions function and start believing in yourself. Addressing the violence is not going to help you in anyway if you do not want to take a stand for yourself.

Always remember that you have been abused for no particular reason. Your self-esteem has been shattered by someone who is among the worst forms of human beings. You never deserved to live with him, but it was the bad choice you made once because of which you are. Remind yourself that you have suffered more than enough, but not anymore. Say to yourself that you of all people deserve better things in life. You deserve all the happiness and blessings of God, and no body, not even your abusive partner, can stop you from achieving your end goals. You are an incredibly talented person and you deserve better; that is the message you need to keep on repeating to yourself.

Reminiscing about how your life was back then when your abusive partner did not come into your life will also make you realize your true worth. At times, society might fail to understand you as a person and what your moral values are in life. But you would personally know yourself much better and right now, only you can help yourself in getting out of this toxic life. Literally no one deserves to be abused in any way, shape, or form. This is your life, and you have a full right to spend it in the happiest way possible.

Intimate partner violence is going to decrease gradually, but would not stop once and for all. There will always be people who want to abuse others, and there will be the innocent ones who will get abused. You cannot possibly change this reality as life can be unfair at a number of times. However, it is in your own hands to take a step forward towards making your life less abusive. This is the least you could do for your own interests before it gets too late.

By saying that you deserve better makes it is understandable that you are not at fault when you were being abuse. Regardless, you are still are not at fault for this abuse. You made a few erroneous decisions in life and fell into the trap of an abusive relationship, but now you know what you have to do in order to get back on track.

In addition to that, some of the reasons behind why you deserve better are listed down below;

- **You need to understand that the abuser is mentally ill and will not stop abusing you.**

The abuser is mentally ill. They are reluctant to become dominant over you by being aggressive and abusive whenever they want to. As soon as you will understand that what your partner is doing is illegal and unfair, you will be able to get out of this situation before something worse happens.

Sometimes, abusers exhibit power and control over you in order to manipulate you and make you feel timid. This is exactly what you should refrain from and ask yourself if you deserve this kind of abusive behavior or not. In this way, you will realize that what you are doing to yourself is just as wrong as what the abuser is doing to you. This needs to stop because this is not what you were born for. You were born to live your life in the best way possible, rather than letting it become more toxic in the hands of others.

• This relationship is not worth it.

Someone who would not value you or show love towards you is not worth doing so much for. A person cannot possibly normalize the ignorant behavior of others just for the clarification. Similarly, you are *not* supposed to stick up with someone who is degrading and belittling you with every passing minute. Domestic violence is a complex issue and you need to understand that being a part of it is going to harm you even more. By staying in an abusive relationship, you will let the abuser know that what he or she is doing is not wrong and you are fine with the way things have been so far.

Before your partner gets this impression that what they are doing is justified, ask yourself if this relationship is worth tolerating the domestic violence or not.

- **There are much better things to do in life rather than staying with a person who is abusive, as well as a control freak.**

Many women in households are being violated domestically and this is not normal at all. There is no doubt that there are a lot of things to experience in life, but holding onto the abusive ones is a mistake being made on your end.

It is pretty obvious that if the victim really wanted to let go of the toxic relationship, they would have to prevent it in the first place. Without moving on in life, how are you supposed to stay out of the trap of being abused? If you will not plan your future beyond the abusive world you are a part of, how are you going to survive and become happy?

It is true to say that there are much better things to do in life. You can actually start over, and that would still be much better than getting abused. When you will plan on leaving the toxic relationship, the abuser will also realize that he has taken you for granted and should have never taken you for such. Soon, the abuser will lose power and control over you, and this is how you will win the fight you have been fighting for a long period of time.

• You deserve better than getting isolated and restricted to behave in a certain way.

What your partner is doing is totally unacceptable, but if you are not doing anything to save yourself from being in the company of such a person, then this is unacceptable as well. Change starts from inside and you deserve everything that is the best in this world. The moment you will realize that being isolated is going to make you more hopeless, you will be open to a positive form of change in your life.

All you need right now is self-awareness, which can only increase if you want to give your life one more chance. This change is the most important step as it will let the abuser know that you cannot be forced or abused anymore. You need to tell them that they cannot put restrictions on you financially, sexually, physically, and mentally. Through this change in your mentality, every single person, including yourself, will know that you deserve better and nobody can stop you from living your life to the fullest.

- **If you will not step out of it, the abuse will escalate and become permanent after some time.**

When the abuser become controlling, he shows dominance over you and if you will not realize what is happening to you, then such abusive behavior will get reinforced. Step out of it before it gets too late and the abuser becomes more aggressive towards you. Being in an abusive relationship is another taboo issue that is not discussed openly among the friends and family members of the victim. The victim might be too afraid to talk about it openly, referring to it as a personal matter of the family. This is utterly wrong as when you will take it lightly, others will do the same and the abuse will escalate.

After some time, you will become accustomed to the abuse and torture, which is the most unwise thing you could ever do in your life. Know that it will get worse with the passage of time, so you have to step out of it right now.

The debate over why you deserve something better is never-ending. Hence, it is your one and only chance to bring change in your life by knowing the true worth of yourself. Instead of letting the abuser take full control over you, decide what is best for you and make it happen as soon as possible. You deserve someone who treats you with love and affection, not someone who never misses a single chance to belittle you in front of others.

You deserve someone who will love your flaws and accept you just the way you are. You are supposed to be with someone who will take good care of you and will never stop doing that. You deserve to be with someone who will respect your decisions and will give you the liberty to make one. You deserve to have someone who will keep on valuing you and will find ways to strengthen your relationship.

Not a single person on this planet wants to be abused in a brutal manner by another human in whom they put their trust. So believe in yourself and get a hold on your life as you are the true owner, not the abuser. Acknowledge the courage you have hidden somewhere inside of you and let it out without giving it a second thought. This is your life and you deserve better, so take a risk and make your life's decisions confidently. Anything can be better than staying in a toxic relationship and compromising your happiness over feelings of constant fear and confusion.

Make sure nobody mistreats you from now on and say to yourself that *"you deserve better"*, because you really do.

Even if you are confused about where to start from, educate yourself and learn more about the domestic violence which you have been facing so far. Just know that you deserve better, and the doors will open on their own. You will be guided through the light coming from those doors and things will sort out on their own. However, this is only possible if you start telling yourself that what is happening to you is intolerable and you deserve anything but violence of this, or any, kind.

You deserve to be respected humanely and your children also (if there are any) deserve to live a happy life in a safe environment. It is your right to feel safe and happy, rather than the current state of your relationship.

"Dedicate yourself to the good you deserve and desire for yourself. Give yourself peace of mind. You deserve to be

happy. You deserve delight."

-Mark Victor Hansen

In the upcoming chapter, we will be studying about why now is the right time to leave this abusive, suffocating relationship.

Chapter 6
It's Time To Go

"Letting go means to come to the realization that some people are a part of your history, but not a part of your destiny."

-Steve Maraboli

Now is the right time to go because it will never happen unless you step up and go. The problem that many women in these situations face is that they are afraid to start their lives over from scratch again. This fear is the fear of the unknown, because they do not know what will happen next. The time to go will never come if you keep on waiting for the right time or for things to become worse. You cannot set a benchmark in such a situation and say that I will leave when something like this happens. You need to stop thinking about going and just go. This is the only way anyone can get out of an abusive relationship. Of course, this will be extremely difficult as there are no set guidelines or steps to take in order to leave your abusive partner; you have to make your own steps and work your own way.

The abuser in question will never stop abusing you once he gets used to it. After getting used to it, they make it a norm to take out their rage, anger and frustration on you. You must accept that the abuser will never change. The problem that women face is that when a woman loves a man, she does it with all her heart.

For this reason, they always believe and see their man as a good person who might do bad things, but eventually comes around and makes them feel better. Yes, the abuser does tend to make up for the abuse, but he does that only to decrease the guilt of hitting his significant other. It is not actually to make the woman feel better. Rather, it is to make themselves feel better.

There are situations, especially in relationships, where a woman tends to think emotionally, but you should not let this get in the way of your thinking. Emotions block your logical thinking and make you do things that normally, a person would never do or endure. Love is the factor that brings emotions in the way of thinking of women. When this '*love*' takes over, they tend to think more about the betterment of their abusive partner. They feel that it is their duty as their partner to help them in overcoming their mental illness in any possible way. What they do not realize is that such men may never recover and may keep on abusing them for the rest of their lives.

What women need to do is to stop thinking about their abusive partner, and start thinking about their happiness. The problem is that they do not think about themselves, their self-esteem, or their children for that matter. When a woman starts thinking emotionally, everything that they can think of leads them towards helping their partner. Women must realize that it is not their duty to cope up with the mental problems of their partners if they are abusing them in any way. Women also have their rights, and nothing gives a man the right to abuse a women in any manner. It is simply inhumane to abuse someone, let alone letting yourself be abused by someone.

You need to think about yourself and what you want from life. All women should get certain basic things from life, such as happiness and an ease of mind. She should not be afraid that her partner will abuse her if she did this or that. They should have confidence that their partner will never become abusive, even if they did something wrong or made a mistake. Such a relationship is healthy, but a relationship where abuse is common is not healthy at all; neither for the women, nor for her children.

You need to get out of an abusive relationship as soon as the abuse starts. No women should have to face an abusive relationship, and yet it is a fact that many women face domestic violence. Moreover, most of them cannot even speak up about it because it is not the norm. In the West, women are speaking up and getting out of relationships if they do not work out, but in the third world countries, women still have to endure domestic abuse without speaking up about it. Even if they do speak up, other people ask them to stay quiet and hope for the things to get better on their own. They might get better in the future, but till that time, the damage will be done and the tainted relationship might never recover from that point onwards. It will eventually become frustrating to live with such a person for the rest of your life.

Women must realize that abusive men will never change and they will continue to abuse them in any manner that they can. That is just the nature of such men because they are mentally ill. A person who is mentally ill may get some advice from psychologists, but they never get around and changing completely. They might stop abusing their partner for some time, but with time it comes back. If you can, you should stop abuse from the first time it takes place. But if you cannot, then it is fruitless to try to cope with it, along with everything else.

Your partner will just keep on looking for excuses to abuse you, never thinking about what it will do to you mentally, or his own children for that matter. When they become angry, they cannot see anything else except for their anger, and when anger takes over, a man does not even think about his children, let alone his partner. No woman deserves such a man, and no child should live with watching their mother get beaten up every other day.

If you cannot get out of the relationship for your own sake, then do it for your children. Children who grow up watching domestic abuse in their homes develop a lot of psychological problems. Such children face a lot of problems further down the road. They grow up watching abusive behavior and hence, tend to become abusive themselves as well. Even if they do not turn out to be an abusive person, they will still face other mental problems.

No matter what happens, you must find a way to get out of this abusive relationship. It is not at all healthy for anyone involved. The real problem that women face is the threat to their lives; like how I had a gun pointed to my face while the police were chasing the car my partner was driving, with me in it. Not every women is as lucky as I am. Then again, I have realized that luck alone has got nothing to do with it because it might be that luck is at your doorstep, giving you an opportunity to get out, but you are not mentally prepared to leave your partner. As a result, you will never realize that there is an opportunity and you will let it go to waste. So the important thing is to convince yourself that it is time to go.

You will realize that it is time to go when you recognize that your partner does not want to change or help themselves. Women think that they can help their abusive partner, but they do not realize that their partner does not wish to be helped. Most women are very naïve because of the innocence of their heart and they think that their love will eventually win them over and change their partner for the good. The reality is that it does not ever happen. No matter how much love you shower at your abusive partner, he will always return it with hatred, anger, and abusive behavior.

Another problem that women face is that they think about their partner's past and the things that have made him the way he is; such as whether their partner has been hurt in the past, which is resulting in this abusive behavior. They think that they can change this abusive behavior if they just go along with it for some time, and love their partner and show them love. This is with the intent that eventually, their partner will turn over a new leaf. Sorry to break this to you, but this never happens.

I have been through many abusive relationships, not just one, so I can tell you that if a person is abusive, it means that the damage to their mental health has been done and they cannot recover back from it and become a normal person who loves and cares for their partner. Because after all the abuse, even the women starts thinking that they are getting exactly what they deserve and that they do not deserve a better life.

This leads to depression, and depression eventually leads to suicide. Even I thought about suicide for quite some time before realizing the importance of my life. When I did, I moved to my mom's house, and of course, my aunt also helped by calling the police that night. What I am trying to tell you is that if you will not help yourself, no one will. You need to stand up for yourself and think about yourself as an individual person, and then decide what you want to do.

When you do decide to go, you should just start acting in that direction without thinking about the consequences. After all, how worse can the situation get when a woman is being abused regularly from time to time. The worst that can happen is that the abusive partner will be so enraged that he might end up killing his partner. Even in such a situation, he will definitely go to prison or worse, as long as the police get a hold of him. Your children will eventually be moved to your parents' house for upbringing, and that is the best case scenario as they might be left without a familiar face as a guardian.

In this way, your children will grow up without either of their parents. Any sane person can see that it is better for children to grow up with their mothers alone if their father is abusive and does not care for his children. Dragging the relationship for the sake of your children's security will never work because eventually, the children might start hating their father for bringing them up in such an environment. So it is far better that you just decide to go and leave with your children.

There are many ways in which a women can just go, leaving their abusive partner alone. You can easily figure out a time of the day when your partner will not be around and will not come back for some time. When you have figured out the time, do not think about your fast paced beating heart; just think about what you have decided and act upon it. Pack the important things if you have time, otherwise just leave everything behind and go with your children. It is okay to be afraid; it is human nature to be afraid of the unknown. Things can be bought later on, but your life cannot come back, so stop being afraid and step out.

In your situation, you will think of many things. What will you do, how you will earn and provide your children with a healthy life style, how you will feed your children, who will take care of you, who will look after things if something terrible happens, and more. Thinking of these things will never solve anything for you. These things will just create a hindrance in the way of your departure from this abusive relationship. If you keep on thinking about it, you will never go. Things have a way of happening and coming around; just believe in yourself that you can do it on your own.

Another problem that makes women think in this way is that they are always taken care of by someone or the other. When they are young, their father is there to look after them, then friends add to protecting them to some extent as well. Not to mention that if you have any siblings, they will look after you as well; at least for some time being if not forever.

Women do not live their lives as independently as men do, which is why they tend to think that they need someone to take care of them. That is why they are afraid to do things on their own after living more than half of their lives being dependent on someone or the other. In comparison, women who do not have anyone to take care of them from the start are more independent and do not think in that way because they believe in themselves and know that they can do it alone as well. You should always look up to such women and take their example as an ideal figure if you want to leave your partner and go. They will give you more inspiration and guts to actually go on about it and leave.

Looking at examples of other women, you will be motivated to make your own move and believe me, once you get out of the abusive relationship that you are in, everything else will automatically settle down one after the other and eventually, you will live peacefully and happily.

Take my own situation as an example; I had nothing when I left my partner and came to live with my mom, except for the support and love of my mother and friends. But with time, I learned to live with my past, and not just that, I also became successful and even my children are living their lives the way I wanted them to live.

I started working online by giving advices to other women who are facing similar problems to what I was facing; an abusive relationship. Slowly and gradually, I started contacting more women who would open up and take my advice, and now I do not only own my own business, but I also have a foundation that works to provide financial and other support to women who chose to leave their partner and start living their lives again.

In order to make you feel better about yourself, I will elaborate a bit more about how I got started with my online business and how it expanded slowly and gradually. I started my own company, Pretty Gurlsz Hu$tle LLC, and in the start, I had nothing to do so I kept on posting everywhere about my company and how I could help other women because I have been through abusive relationships as well. I was hoping to get some responses right away, but as it turned out, I had nothing to do even after a few months.

Then, a girl contacted me and we started talking, and while she told me about herself and I shared my experience with her, I realized that it made me feel much better about myself too. I thought to myself that if helping one girl can make me feel like this, then how better will I feel if I had dozens of women to help? And so, I never gave up and kept pursuing women, even if they did not want to open up. I told them about myself and my story to make them feel more comfortable, and it worked. So you do not need to worry about what you will do, because eventually you will do something or the other to make your life beautiful.

Another problem that is faced by women is that they keep on pretending that everything is fine, and after some time, they start believing it too. This can make you mentally ill as well, and you can easily go into depression. At this point, your children will suffer the most because their father does not care about them and your depression will stop you from thinking straight and helping your children in their lives. They will feel left alone and they will also feel guilty about not being able to help their mother, and at the same time they will also feel that their mother is doing nothing to help herself and her children.

The biggest problem that I have realized women face is to actually leave their partner. This is the most crucial point and if you do not stop yourself from thinking about your partner and how much you both love each other, which may not even be true really, you will never be able to go.

As I have emphasized earlier, women tend to think more emotionally than rationally in certain situations, especially when they are on the verge of leaving their partner. This is when their past flashes in front of them, and the amazing thing is that, when women think about their past, their mind somehow skips all the bad things and reminds them of all the good things in their relationships. Thereby, putting more weight towards wanting to stay, rather than to leave. If you can just control your thoughts in that moment, you will go and live your life happily with your children, provided that you have children.

To sum it all up, I would first remind you once more that if you keep on thinking about going and what you will do if you do leave, then you will never be able to leave. So just stop thinking about everything else and think about leaving in that present moment. Do not let your thoughts wander off into the future, or it will scare you away. That is just the way it works, so do not sweat on it.

Think about your own self-esteem. Think that you are beautiful and do not deserve this relationship. Think about your children and their future's potential. Think about anything that will contribute towards making the decision to go, and just go. Do not look back, do not think about your partner, and do not think that he will be left alone without even the children because honestly, such a man does not deserve to live happily with a family.

Chapter 7

Forgive And Forget

"Sooner or later we've all got to let go of our past."

-Dan Brown

Once you have moved away and successfully escaped that toxic relationship, it is time to create a new and healthy relationship that is built on intimacy and mutual support. There is nothing wrong in moving forward with your life and this should be your only goal at the moment. We often associate negative ideas with moving ahead in life and focus on living an isolated life. This is one of the unhealthiest things you could do to yourself.

You have come so far and now, you need to move ahead instead of holding any grudges against a past relationship. No doubt it was nothing compared to your other hardships and struggles, but if you will not let go of the past, you will never stop living in the prison of your past memories. Emotionally and physically, try to build up yourself as much as possible since you have an open ground available. You have escaped the past and nobody stopped you then, so why should you hold yourself back now?

All you need is some courage to move on and once you will decide to make your life better, you will start achieving goals. Having said that, you should also remember that regardless of the frightening experience you have had, isolation is not the answer. Moving on can be done in many ways and one of the most effective ways would be possible by engaging with people who are positive in every aspect.

You have been in a secluded environment for a long period of time and you surely did not deserve anything even remotely close to that. Now that you are out of it, you need to start mingling with people who will make your life easier and happier.

By staying in an abusive relationship, you have missed out on the basic necessities of life. Freedom to live happily and deciding what to do on your own is a blessing in disguise. People who have run away from abusive relationships can understand the value of freedom and will forever cherish living their life in their own way.

The victims of domestic abuse do not get to interact with other people besides the abuser himself, and this makes them more dependent on their partner. However, after getting out of this toxic relationship, they get to experience things they deserved, but could not do so unfortunately. When we talk about getting out of domestic violence, we need to address it in the best way possible. This is a huge step which you have taken already, and the rest comes with managing your life and making it better with the passage of time. You were a victim of stress, and eventually depression, but luckily this pattern is going to change from your side. Down below are some of the most effective ways of moving forward in life by following the policy of *'forgive and forget'*.

First Things First, Try Regaining Your Self-Worth And Self-Confidence

Breaking away from an abusive relationship has its own benefits, like regaining the long lost self-confidence you once had. Surely you were confident enough to take the most important step of your life, of running away from the domestic violence. If you can take such a stand for yourself, you can conquer anything in this world. This is one of the best examples of how confident you are and that you put yourself first, instead of the abusive relationship.

Self-worth and self-confidence gets shattered when someone you trusted makes you feel worthless. By staying with such an abusive person who never valued you, you get torn apart and stop valuing yourself. Gradually, you start losing your self-confidence and become accustomed to the kind of mistreatment you have been facing since years.

Although, the time has come to finally move on and leave everything else behind, you need to focus on your own nourishment and this calls for regaining your self-confidence and self-worth. In this way, you will get a good dose of encouragement to turn your lost dreams into a reality and accomplish your goals. You can plan on doing things you have not done before or keep things as simplistic as you can.

All of this totally depends on you from now on as you are the one who is going to decide how to move forward. The more confident you will be, the better a decision maker you will become. The decisions you will take for yourself can never go wrong if you trust yourself and have a belief that the good times will come anytime soon.

Now you are free to dream again and do whatever you feel like. This is the privilege you always deserved and now is the right time to bring out your inner confidence and feel alive. You have every right to plan the best life for yourself and this would not be possible if you will hold on to your past. If you value yourself, you will plan on moving ahead and keeping your priorities straight.

The best way to do that will be planning the things you always wanted to do and achieving those goals one by one. Not only your confidence will boost up, but you will notice the positive change in your overall personality.

These goals can be as simple as you want them to be, like talking to a stranger or going grocery shopping on your own. You can order a pizza to treat yourself after accomplishing those goals and this way, you will realize your own worth. As long as you are happy and satisfied with your present life, you will not have to do much to regain your confidence. This confidence of yours of standing up for yourself shows how much you have progressed so far in this healing process. If you have not put yourself first and realized your worth, you would not have been able to make it this far in life. So keep your confidence levels on track and you are good to move forward in your journey of recovery.

Interact With The Kind Of People Who Will Make You Happier And Have A Brighter Outlook On Life

One thing which needs to be changed is the fact that people isolate themselves after getting out of the abusive relationship. This is an unhealthy act and you clearly do not deserve to live your life in dismay. Moving ahead by forgetting and forgiving is an essential part of your healing process and you need to acknowledge its significance.

Often times, we would not feel like talking to anybody just because of the trust issues we developed through our previous abusive relationship. But to recover, you need to get out of the past and live your life. That is the whole essence of stepping up and taking charge.

So try to engage yourself with people who will take care of you. There are good people out there who will understand the trials you have gone through and will surely be a part of your journey in moving towards a healthier life. But first, you will have to open up yourself a little bit and make space for others.

The majority of these victims get out of touch with their loved ones when being in an abusive relationship. They lose contact with them because of their partner, which makes their life even more miserable. However, after getting out of the abusive relationship, you are free to explore the bonds left behind and have the best time of your life.

Human relations have always played a vital role in strengthening bonds among people. For that reason, interacting with the right people will bring out a positive side of yours and you will notice a blossoming change in your life. Having conversations with the positive minded people, your closest friends and family members will be good for your well-being and the memories of your past will fade over time.

Another important relationship that you have to keep in mind while moving ahead is the future of your love life. The thought of dating can be daunting after your past experience, but it is necessary. As we said earlier, a part of this healthy progress into the future is building healthy relationships. You need to forgive and forget the past. Learn from the past and use it to find a better intimate relationship.

Hopefully, now that you are thinking about dating I should also tell you one important thing. Give yourself time. Take all the time in the world before you jump into the dating pool. This cannot be a hasty decision, because trusting another individual again can be an enormous task. So wait till you are able to once again embrace the intimacy of another individual.

As you move ahead, just make sure that you do not let the past effect your present or future in anyway. Have fun with people you deeply care for and take charge of your life. You have enough in your regretful past, but your future is still out there, waiting for you to explore it. So go out there with a positive mind and have fun with the type of people you are comfortable around. This is similar to having a bright outlook towards the new life you have found, so you should grab this opportunity with both hands.

Just do not stop hoping for the best and stay optimistic for as long as you can. The end results will pour in and your life will escape the shackles of the abusive relationship you were once a part of.

Lastly, Keep Yourself Occupied With Tasks That Will Make You A Better Human

Being in abusive relationship stops you from thinking straight. The victim gets so mentally disturbed that they hardly pay attention to their mental and physical health. However, after getting rid of the toxic person, you are supposed to forgive and move on. If you will not forget your past, you will remain stuck in it and this will take you nowhere in life. You have left that abusive lifestyle for a reason and now, you are only going to hurt yourself by thinking about it.

Therefore, your mind should be preoccupied with positive and self-nourishing thoughts. Thoughts that will make you feel good about yourself and will help you live a life you have always dreamt of.

How you think now will be influential for your overall lifestyle, so try to occupy yourself with thoughts and ideas that will make you love your present life. I do not want you to think about what happened in the past. Your past should remain where it is supposed to and all your focus should be on the future at the moment.

This is a part of your recovery process, so try not to play around with it. This victory of letting go of the abusive relationship is earned by very few people and you are the lucky one, so let it be the way it is. Look ahead to what life will bring you and forget whatsoever went wrong.

An effective way to do so will be going to the recovery classes where you will heal by seeking advice from experts. Yes, there are many volunteering classes being held for the victims of domestic violence. You can go to these classes and seek for further help. Rather than wasting your time on figuring out things, taking these classes will help you out and make you identify your vision in life with clarity.

You need to become stronger and take control over your life, and these therapeutic classes will be a good way of achieving that. Through these classes, you can easily reevaluate your coping strategies. Most importantly, you will learn to forgive yourself.

Some of the coping strategies that you can resort to are planning out your future. Engage yourself in things you feel good about and allow you to get closer with yourself. For example, if you are a writer, you can work on becoming more positive by speaking up about the domestic violence. Channel your negative feelings towards something positive and enlightening. Try to use your voice to influence others and bring a positive impact in not only their lives, but yours as well.

Coming out of the toxic relationship will provide you with a new perspective of life and you will see how much you have been ignored. Now is the time to make up for any regrets you had in the past and move forward in an enthusiastic manner.

No matter how hard it is to forget traumatic experiences you have faced, sooner or later you will have to let go. No good came to you when you were in an abusive relationship, and the same will happen if you will continue to overthink it. Your mind needs to grow out of this experience in order to accept the new changes in life and engross yourself even more with positive thoughts.

Once the fog starts to lift, you will see the things you have not paid attention to in the past. You will change for the better and live your life in a whole new way. You are here to fix your wounds and forget the trials and tribulations you were engrossed with. You are here to stay happy, and tell others to do the same.

You are an exemplary figure for others who are going through the same thing, so try to spread a positive message. When you will understand this, others will try to follow in your path and get out of the little bubble they have reserved themselves with.

Instead of crying over the spilt milk, avail this incredible chance at living an independent and happier life. Use this opportunity to follow the career you always wanted. As soon as you will incorporate the *'forgive and forget'* policy in your life, you will realize the insurmountable benefits of your decision. You will be grateful for not holding on to your past relationships and soon, you will be telling others to do the same. Who knows, you might be able to stop others from becoming victims of the deadly abuse you were once a victim of.

This is exactly what I am doing right now. I am trying my best to help others get out of their abusive relationships as I do not want others to go through the abuse I have faced in my life. I know from my own experience that learning to move on is not as difficult as we are taught it is. Do not hesitate for a moment longer; the moment you see an opportunity, seize it and move on. Take this initiative, and the world will automatically bend itself in your favor to help you recover.

Bibliography

Do Not Be A Victim of Care Abuse (2016) Retrieved from http://www.aardvarc.org/

BROKEN2BLESSED

Made in the USA
Middletown, DE
15 February 2022

61207541R10068